Joke Book For Funny Jokes for 13-17 Year Olds

Geordan Richardson

©. Geordan Richardson. 2023.

All rights reserved.

No part of this publication may be reproduced without consent from the copyright holder.

Hi there!

Thanks for buying our book!

If you enjoy it please feel free to leave a review.

Instagram: @zoomer_publishing

Twitter: @geordan2003

Zoomer Publishing is an independent publishing brand run by independent author Geordan Richardson.

We produce books in a variety of different niches for Generation Z.

We understand the problems Gen Z faces in the world today, with one being a limited ability to focus and a short attention span.

We believe reading can be a significant remedy for this and want our books to be a source of good in the lives of Gen Z.

We publish books that Gen Z can learn from, enjoy and above all else; help Gen Z.

Follow us on Instagram, TikTok and Twitter to keep updated with new releases.

One of my most recent books is a crucial one for Generation Z. 'How To Improve Your Social Media Habits.'

Scan the below QR code to claim a free e-book and audio sample!

Table of Contents

What Do You Call A... Jokes? 10

Knock-Knock Jokes 15

School Jokes 20

General Jokes 27

What Do You Call A... Jokes?

What do you call a bear with no teeth?

A gummy bear!

What do you call a snowman with six-pack abs?

An 'abdominal' snowman!

What do you call a dinosaur with an extensive vocabulary?

A thesaurus!

What do you call an alligator in a vest?

An investigator!

What do you call a snowman on a hot day?

A puddle!

What do you call a fish wearing a suit?

Sofishticated!

What do you call a test tube?

A graduated cylinder!

What do you call a cat who sits on the beach on Christmas Eve?

Sandy Claws!

What do you call an obnoxious reindeer?

Rude-olph!

What do you call security guards who work outside Samsung shops?

Guardians of the Galaxy!

Knock-Knock Jokes

Knock, knock.

Who's there?

Beats.

Beats who?

Beats me! I don't know!

Knock, knock

Who's there?

Goat.

Goat who?

Goat to the door now, c'mon I'm waiting outside!

Knock, Knock

Who's there?

Noah

Noah who?

Noah good place to go to dinner?

Knock, Knock

Who's there?

Shore

Shore who?

Shore hope I am let in soon!

Knock, Knock

Who's there?

Boo

Boo Who?

Don't cry it's only a joke!

Knock, Knock

Who's there?

Weirdo

Weirdo Who?

Weirdo you think you're going?!

Knock, Knock

Who's there?

Nobel

Nobel who?

There is Nobel... this is why I knocked!

Knock, Knock

Who's there?

Ice Cream

Ice Cream who?

Ice Cream so you can hear me!

School Jokes

My old college girlfriend asked for my help with her algebra homework

Unfortunately I don't solve for ex!

In school, our family was so broke we couldn't pay our electricity bills

Those were the darkest days of our lives!

Why did the music note drop out of college?

Because it couldn't pick a major!

Define an optimist.

A college student who opens his wallet and expects to find money!

How do you flirt with a math teacher?

Use an acute angle!

What do you get if you cross a student and an alien?

Someone from a university!

What did the music thief do in college?

Take notes!

In college, I lived on a houseboat and started seeing the girl next door.

Eventually, we drifted apart!

Why shouldn't you write with a broken pencil?

Well... it's pointless!

Why was 6 afraid of 7?

Because 7, 8, 9!

What's the scariest word in nuclear physics?

Oops!

Why aren't you worried about passing math?

Why should I be? It's as easy as pi!

Why did the sun skip college?

Because it already has a million degrees!

What is 56+6-8+67+999-111?

A headache!

Why did the sun go to school?

To get brighter

What made the math book sad?

It had 'two' many problems!

How do bees get to school?

By the school buzz!

General Jokes

Finally, I announced to my hot co-worker how I felt. Thankfully she felt the same way.

So I turned on the air conditioning!

I have an incredible date for Valentine's Day.

February 14th!

My wife keeps telling me that I'm the cheapest person she has ever met in her life.

I'm not buying it!

What did the frustrated cat say?

Are you kitten me right meow!

Why was the candle happy?

It was liit!

Why didn't the sesame seed leave the casino?

It was on a roll!

I once fell in love with a girl who only knew 4 vowels.

She didn't know I existed!

RIP to boiling water…

You will be mist!

Why do you want to work in the mirror category?

I dunno, I just see myself doing it!

What's a can opener that doesn't work?

A can't opener!

My friends always prefers the stairs, whereas I always choose to take the lift.

I guess we were raised differently!

What keeps the ocean clean?

Mer-maids!

What do you get from a pampered cow?

Spoiled milk!

What's red and bad for your teeth?

A brick!

I have many jokes about unemployed people.

Sadly, none of them work!

What will always rise and never drop?

Your age!

Why was it so windy at the football match?

The stands were packed with fans!

How come squares don't talk to circles?

Why would they? There's no point!

Why did the skeletons quit their jobs?

Because their hearts weren't in it!

Where do vampires wash themselves?

In a blood bath!

What did the astronaut say when he crashed the satellite?

I Apollo-gize!

Why wouldn't you tell a window a joke?

Well, it would just crack up!

What happened to the two thieves who stole a calendar?

Oh yeah, they got six months each!

What did the DNA strand say to another DNA strand?

Hey, how do these genes look on me!

What is ant called who fights crime?

A vigilante!

What is a funny mountain called?

Hill-arious!

How come the broom was running late?

It over-swept!

What did the mobile phone do to propose to his girlfriend?

He gave her a ring!

What travels around the world but will always stay in a corner?

A stamp!

Why are robots never afraid?

They have nerves of steel!

How come weightlifters are always annoyed?

Because they always have to work with dumbbells!

Brilliant! My refrigerator is working!

Careful, you better catch it before you run away!

Which is faster? Hot or cold?

Hot. Because you can easily catch a cold!

When can a door not actually be a door?

When it's ajar!

What is the computer's favourite snack?

Computer chips!

What lion will never roar?

A dandelion!

Where did the sheep go on holidays?

The Baa-hamas!

What can't you throw but are always able to catch?

A cold!

What has more letters than the alphabet?

The post office!

What runs around a field but never moves?

A fence!

Where did you learn to make ice creams?

Sundae school!

How are magicians and footballers similar?

They can both do hat tricks!

What time do the ducks wake up?

The quack of dawn!

What is your favourite day to go to the beach?

Sun-day!

What is a belt with a watch on it?

A waist of time!

Which part of the eye is the most hardworking?

The pupil!

What type of tea is always hard to swallow?

Reali-tea!

What's the best way to burn 1000 calories?

Leave the chips and burgers in the oven!

Why can't pirates learn the alphabet?

Because they got lost at 'C'!

Why are spiders so intelligent?

Because they are always surfing on the web!

What type of music do balloons hate?

Pop!

Why did the man fall into the hole?

He couldn't see that well!

Is February able to March?

No, but April May!

How many tickles does it take to make an octopus laugh?

Ten-tickles!

How come aliens don't want to celebrate Christmas?

They don't like to give away their presence!

What do snowmen eat for their breakfast?

Snowflakes!

I told my family I graduated from circus college

They all laughed at me!

What would you call a greedy elf?

Elfish!

What will always fall but never get hurt?

Snow!

My girlfriend left a note at my brand new Porsche. It said, "This is not working!" I got nervous.

I started the car and it is working fine!

I just opened a new flower shop.

Business is blooming!

How do sheep celebrate the 4th of July?

With a baa-baa-cue!

How does the sun listen to music?

On a ray-dio!

Why are lovers like dandruff?

I just cannot get you out of my head no matter how hard I try!

What did the magnet say to the fridge?

You're very attractive!

Why should you never break up with a goalie?

Because he's a keeper!

How can a spy catch a cold?

If he isn't undercover!

Why did the football team go undercover?

To get their quarterback!

My sister hates it when I invade her privacy.

I learned this when I read her diary!

My friend lost his tongue in a bad accident.

I was going to make a joke but thought it would be quite tasteless!

What will always fall but never get hurt?

Snow!

Why don't cars work after you change their wheels?

Because they are retired!

Why did the basketball player bring a stepladder to his match?

Because he wanted to reach new heights!

How do penguins build their house?

Igloos them together!

Did you hear about the claustrophobic astronaut?

Yeah! He just needed a little space!

How about the new restaurant called Karma?

Yeah, did you see the menu?

You get what you deserve!

Where are most average things manufactured?

The satisfactory!

What's so good about visiting Switzerland?

I don't know, but the flag is a big plus!

A bear walks into the bar and says,: 'Can I have a whiskey and a… cola please?' The bartender says: 'Why the long pause?'

The bear replies: 'I don't know. I was born with them.'

A man says to his doctor: 'Doctor, help me I think I am addicted to Instagram!'

The doctor responds: 'Sorry I don't follow you'

Why did the soccer player bring a piece of string to the game?

So he was able to tie the score!

Why might golfers bring two pairs of pants while they are playing?

Because they could get a hole-in-one!

What did the grape say when he got stepped on?

Nothing, he just let out a little whine!

If you cross a shark with a snowman what do you get?

Frostbite!

Why do bees hum?

Because they don't know the words!

What did the hat say to the other hat?

'You stay here… I'll go on ahead.'

Why don't skeletons like fighting each other?

They don't have the guts!

What music do rabbits like to listen to?

Hip-Hop!

What did the left eye say to the right eye?

Between us… something smells!

Why do bees have sticky hair?

Because they use honeycomb!

Why did the bicycle fall over?

Because it was two-tired!

What did the elevator say to the other elevator?

I think I'm coming down with something!

Why can't scientists trust atoms?

Because they make up everything!

What did the wall say to the other wall?

'I'll see you at the corner?'

What happened to the actor who fell through the floorboards?

There was not much, he was just going through a stage!

If I have 20 apples in one hand and 10 oranges in the other hand, what do I have?

Big hands!

What do teenage ducks hate?

Duck quacks!

Why can't you hear a pterodactyl in the bathroom?

It has a silent pee!

I didn't know why the baseball was getting bigger…

Then it hit me!

How come pimples make horrible prisoners?

They keep breaking out!

Why can't a T-Rex clap his hands?

Because they're extinct of course!

Why didn't the snowman want to go to the party?

Because he didn't want to thaw out!

Are you free tomorrow?

Sorry, but I'm expensive!

How come waterbeds are so bouncy?

They're filled with spring water!

Why was the frog forced to call his insurance company?

He had a 'jump' in his car!

Why did the tomato turn red with embarrassment?

Because it saw the salad dressing!

Hi there!

Thanks for reading my book!

If you enjoy it please feel free to leave a review.

Instagram: zoomer_publishing

TikTok: @zoomer.publishing

Printed in Great Britain
by Amazon